No Room at the Inn

FaithPoint PRESS

No Room at the Inn

Nell Navillus

Illustrated by

Jodie McCallum

FaithPoint PRESS

Hezir and Miriam were very busy helping their father run his inn. It was a busy time of year, with crowds of people from all over Judea coming to town, according to the king's decree, to be counted for taxes.

Normally their family inn in Bethlehem was a quiet place. Never before had Hezir or Miriam seen such crowds. They were working overtime, with Mama and Auntie cooking all day and night, and Father and Uncle taking care of the guests' horses and camels and donkeys. Miriam helped keep the inn clean and wait on the guests, and Hezir helped his father and uncle with the animals.

"Bring me some more hot water, Miriam!" Auntie would call out. "Hezir, take these donkeys to the side lot!" Father would command. "Where is that plate of bread and olives?" Mama would demand. "We don't have enough hay!" "Put these two children in your bed!" And so on.

Late one night, when the grownups were busy with the largest crowd ever, there came a knock on the door of the inn. Since everyone else was busy, Miriam answered, calling to her brother to come help her. A family stood at the door, very tired, and dusty from a long journey.

"May I help you?" said Hezir, letting Miriam know with a glance that he would take charge. "Do you have any room for us?" the man before them asked. He wore a brown robe of rough cloth and sandals. He held by a rope a weary little donkey, which bore on its back a lovely woman in blue, who smiled at them. Miriam could see at once that the woman was expecting a baby.

"We're full up," said Hezir. "It seems everyone in Judea wants to lodge here." Miriam added, "There are many other inns in town." The man shook his head. "We've tried everywhere. There are no rooms, and my wife is very tired. She needs to rest." Hezir and Miriam shared a glance. "Let me run and get my papa," Miriam told the young family.

Miriam ran to the central room of the inn, where a few lodgers lingered at their tables, eating her mother's fine lamb stew and nibbling on sweet cookies, and talking with her father. "Papa! You must come!" She tugged at his arm. "All right, what's this about?" Papa joined Hezir at the door where the young couple and their donkey were waiting. "Papa, these people are very tired and there is no place for them to rest!" Hezir said. "Couldn't they spend the night in our stable?"

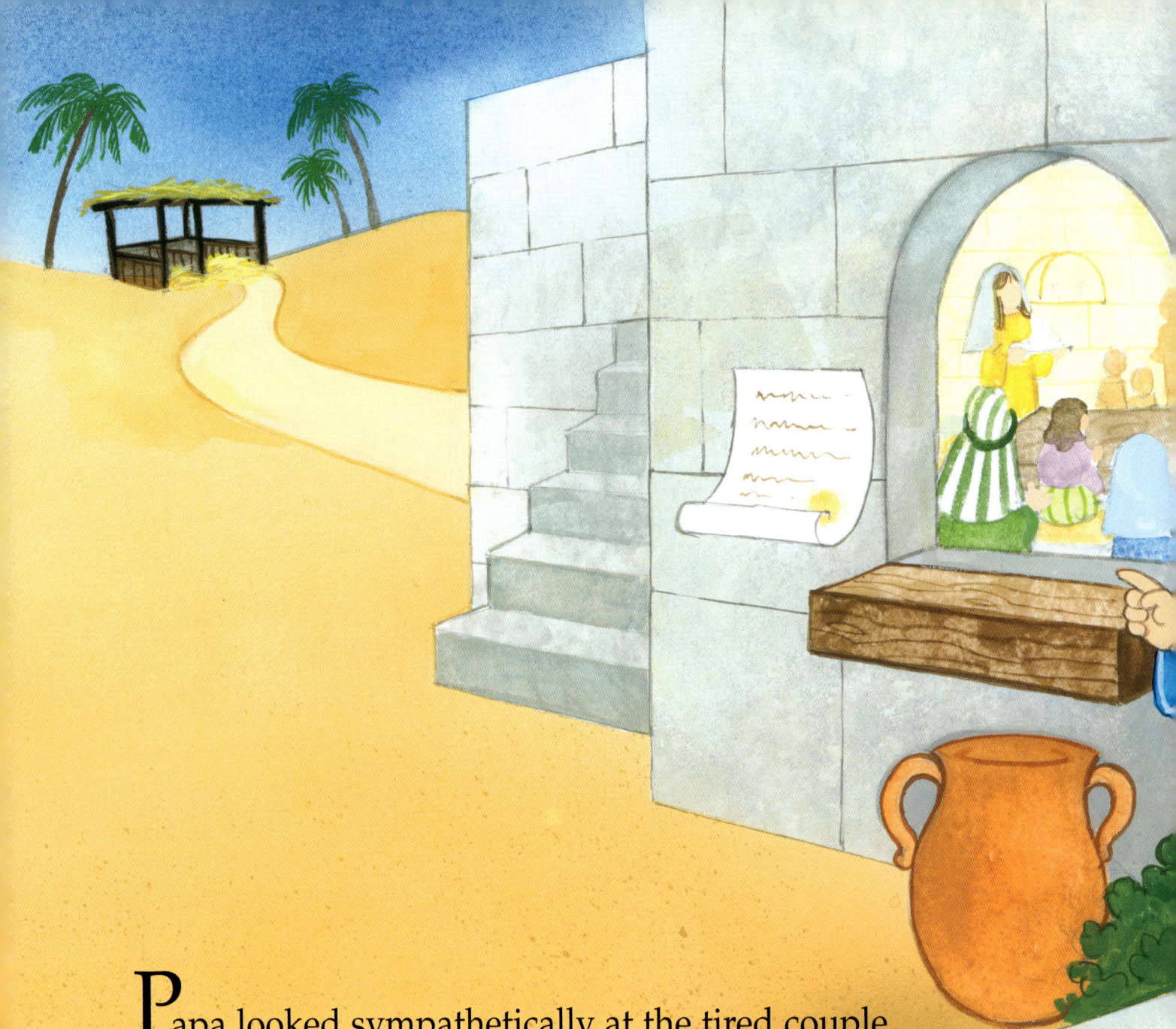

Papa looked sympathetically at the tired couple, but said to Hezir, "It is cold out there, and the stable is filled with animals. It is no place to spend the night." "Please sir," said the man at the door. "My name is Joseph, of Nazareth. This is my wife Mary. She must rest."

Papa smiled. "Very well. Hezir, show Joseph and Mary to the stable.

Miriam, run get some food from your mother. And some blankets for these people. Make it quick!"

And so Joseph and Mary were lodged in the humble stable for the night. Hezir and Miriam went to bed very late. But they couldn't sleep. A brilliant star shown through the window, and there was a strange procession coming down the road, right into their stable yard! Some shepherds came with their sheep, and three exotic men on camels, loaded with baggage. They clustered around the little stable, as if they were looking for something.

"This town really is crowded tonight," Hezir whistled under his breath. He wanted to wake their father up, but Miriam hushed him. "Let's sneak out and see what they want," she whispered. "Then if we need to wake Mama and Papa, we will."

The soft glow of the oil lamps in the stables, and the brightness of the star in the east guided their steps as Miriam and Hezir made their way silently across the yard of the inn. As they approached the cluster of shepherds, they saw the richly dressed men kneeling before the manger and—most amazing of all—there was a beautiful little baby lying there on the straw.

Miriam and Hezir worked their way closer. Joseph, tired but happy, looked up and saw them. Mary smiled. "Come," Joseph waved them over. "See, we have a son." The baby looked at the children then and smiled, and the night was filled with peace.

"Glory be to God!" cried one of the shepherds. "Jesus Christ is born. Let there be peace on earth, and goodwill to men!"

"Amen," said all those around. And God's great love spread across the world from that moment on, bringing Hezir and Miriam and their family, and all people everywhere, everlasting life.